James Perimal

The Birthday Joke Book

Also available from Mammoth

The Creepy Crawly Joke Book
My Funny Valentine
Love and Kisses
The Green and Hairy Joke Book
The Yellow and Highly Dangerous Joke Book
The Holiday Joke Book
The Biodegradable Joke Book

The Birthday Joke Book

Mark Burgess

MAMMOTH

First published in Great Britain 1991 by Mammoth
an imprint of Mandarin paperbacks
Michelin House, 81 Fulham Road, London SW3 6RB

Mandarin is an imprint of the Octopus Publishing Group

Text copyright © Mark Burgess 1990
Illustrations copyright © Mark Burgess 1990

The Jokes on pages 88-91 were the winners of the
Fun Factory Joke Quiz on SKY TV and come from
Damian, the Netherlands; Ann Culbertson, N. Ireland;
Robert Haddington, N. Yorkshire; Sarah Hutson, Greece;
David Rickard, Dublin; Nicola Brookes, Leicestershire; Sarah Wootton,
Staffordshire; Emma Bruen, Dublin; Elisa Boelens, the Netherlands;
and Emma Clark, Buckinghamshire.

ISBN 0 7497 0342 3

A CIP catalogue record for this title
is available from the British Library

Printed in Great Britain
by Cox & Wyman Ltd, Reading, Berkshire

This paperback is sold subject to the condition
that it shall not, by way of trade or otherwise,
be lent, resold, hired out, or otherwise circulated
without the publisher's prior consent in any form
of binding or cover other than that in which
it is published and without a similar condition
including this condition being imposed
on the subsequent purchaser.

BIRTHDAY WISHES

Have you heard the joke about the birthday card that wasn't posted?
You'll never get it.

How do bees wish each other 'Happy Birthday'?
They say it with flowers.

Who gets the sack on his birthday?
A postman.

What do sparrows send their friends for their birthdays?
Birdy cards.

How do you say 'Happy Birthday' to a large and fierce tiger?
From as far away as possible.

What did the rabbit write in the birthday card?
Hoppy Birthday!

How does a pig sign a birthday card?
With pen and oink.

What did the sheep write in the birthday card?
Happy Birthday to ewe.

What's orange and wobbly and sent by the Queen on your 100th birthday?
A jellygram.

What happens on the King of the Rabbits' birthday?
He's given a twenty-one bun salute.

Postman: Is this birthday card for you?
The name's smudged.
Boy: *No, my name's William.*

Fred: My grandad is still alive at 97!
Tom: That's nothing, my grandad is still
alive at 129.
Fred: What, one hundred and twenty-nine?
Tom: Yes – 129 Rhubarb Road.

Why do monkeys never forget birthdays?
They like dates.

'Why were you born in Scunthorpe?'
'To be near my mother.'

If you can tell the age of a tree by its rings, how do you tell the age of a person?
By their wringles.

Have you heard the one about the giraffe that lived to a hundred?
It's a tall story.

How do you wish a fish 'Happy Birthday'?
Drop him a line.

How do you wish a sloth 'Happy Birthday'?
Like This!

How do you wish an African Elephant 'Happy Birthday'?
Make a trunk call.

WAKEY! WAKEY!

Why is getting up at three in the morning on your birthday like a pig's tail?
Because it's twirly.

What do polar bears like for breakfast on their birthdays?
Snowflakes.

What do cats like for breakfast on their birthdays?
Mice crispies.

Why is bread like champagne?
It's good for toasting.

I want a bike that cooks eggs for my birthday
– *A scrambler!*

Did you hear the joke about the eggs?
Two bad.

Two ears of corn were running up a hill. What were they when they reached the top?
Puffed wheat.

Did you hear the one about the cornflakes?
Well, there was this box of cornflakes and – I'll tell you the rest next week as it's a cereal.

How do you make a sausage roll?
Push it.

What's bread?
Raw toast.

How did the monkey make toast?
He put it under a gorilla.

What do witches have for breakfast on their birthdays?
Snap, cackle and pop.

What do ghosts eat for breakfast?
Dreaded wheat.

What does Dracula like for breakfast on his birthday?
Readyneck.

What do Frenchmen have for breakfast on their birthdays?
Huit heures bix.

What do cats like reading on their birthdays?
The Mews of the World.

What do dogs like reading on their birthdays?
Bones and Gardens.

GO BANANAS!

Why was the banana blue?
It forgot the apple's birthday!

What's yellow on the inside and pink with candles on the outside?
A banana disguised as a birthday cake.

Why is a banana like a pullover?
Because it's easy to slip on.

If cobblers make shoes, what do bananas make?
Slippers.

Why doesn't a banana snore?
So it won't wake the rest of the bunch.

What's yellow and points north?
A magnetic banana.

What's yellow and goes 'click, click'?
A ball-point banana.

When is a banana not a banana?
When it's a little hoarse – after singing 'Happy Birthday to You'!

What's yellow and in a tearing hurry?
A banana opening its birthday presents!

KNOCK, KNOCK...

Knock, knock.
Who's there?
Shirley.
Shirley who?
Shirley you invited me to your birthday party?

Knock, knock.
Who's there?
Ivor.
Ivor who?
Ivor gotten your birthday present.

Knock, knock.
Who's there?
Wood.
Wood who?
Wood I forget your birthday?

Knock, knock.
Who's there?
Police.
Police who?
Police let me come to your birthday party.

Knock, knock.
Who's there?
Lettuce.
Lettuce who?
Lettuce in quickly, it's raining.

Knock, knock.
Who's there?
Arthur.
Arthur who?
Arthur any biscuits left?

FUN & GAMES

What do kangaroos like playing at birthday parties?
Hopscotch.

What's out-of-bounds at a birthday party?
An exhausted kangaroo.

What do cannibals play at birthday parties?
Swallow my leader.

Why are crocodiles easy to fool at birthday parties?
They'll swallow anything.

What's a crocodile's favourite game?
Snap.

What do parrots like playing at birthday parties?
Monopolly.

What game do cows like playing?
Moo-sical chairs.

How do you start a teddy-bear race?
Ready, teddy, go!

How do you start a jelly race?
Get set!

How do you start a milk pudding race?
Sago.

Why did the orange stop at the top of the hill?
It had run out of juice.

Why shouldn't you swim on an empty stomach?
Because its easier to swim in the swimming pool.

Why shouldn't you swim if your watch is broken?
Well, you won't have the time.

What kind of sweets are best at games?
Liquorice Allsports.

What do horses like playing at birthday parties?
Stable tennis.

What do mice like playing?
Hide and squeak.

What are chickens best at?
The egg-and-spoon race.

What game do spacemen play on their birthdays?
Astronoughts and crosses.

What do frogs like playing at birthday parties?
Croquet.

What are frogs best at?
Hopscotch (when the kangaroos are all out-of-bounds!)

Why shouldn't you play birthday games in the jungle?
There are too many cheetahs.

How do you start a flea race?
One, two, flea – go!

What do postmen like playing at birthday parties?
Postman's knock.

What game do postmen play best?
Pass the parcel.

PARTY TIME

What do you serve birthday tea to your dog on?
Bone china.

What do pixies like for birthday tea?
Fairy cakes.

Why do pixies have such bad table manners?
They're always goblin.

What do sea monsters like for birthday tea?
Fish and ships.

What's the difference between a monster and an elephant?
A monster never remembers your birthday.

What do cats like at birthday parties?
Chocolate mouse.

What do you call an ant that doesn't know it's your birthday?
Ignorant.

What goes 'Quick, quick' at birthday parties?
A duck with hiccups.

How do you spell 'hungry horse' in four letters?
MTGG.

How do you say 'Happy Birthday' to a monkey with bananas in his ears?
Any way you like – he won't hear you.

Why did the cannibal have to leave the birthday party?
He wanted to toast the host.

What do you do if a rabbit comes to your birthday party uninvited?
Tell him to hop it.

Why shouldn't you invite a herd of cows to your birthday party?
There'd be udder chaos.

Why didn't the camel go to the birthday party?
Because he had the hump.

Why did the skeleton go to the birthday party?
For a rattling good time.

Why is Frankenstein good fun at birthday parties?
'Cos he'll have you in stitches.

'Did the skunks mind not being invited to your birthday party?'
'*Yes, they raised a stink.*'

Why don't boxers like birthday parties?
'Cos they're given the bumps.

'Would you like to come to my birthday party on Saturday, Jill?'
'Thanks, Mike. Where do you live?'
'Number 23, Oxford Road. Just push the bell with your elbow.'
'Why with my elbow?'
'Well, you're not coming empty-handed are you?'

How do you get rid of a cobbler who's come to your birthday party uninvited?
Say 'Shoo'.

'There's a pop group at my birthday party.'
'Where?'
'On the table: two bottles of lemonade and three bottles of coke.'

What does a chicken like on its birthday?
Hentertainment.

Why did the chicken cross the road?
To go to the birdy party.

What do ducks dance at birthday parties?
The Quackstep.

What's the best place for a party on board ship?
Wherever the funnel be.

What do polar bears sing at birthday parties?
'Freeze a jolly good fellow . . .'

What did the astronaut hope for on his birthday?
A special birthday launch.

Why did the MP leave the Houses of Parliament?
He wanted to join the Birthday Party!

Why couldn't the skeleton go to the birthday party?
He had nobody to go with.

My little brother did bird impressions at my birthday party
— *he ate worms.*

What did the bees sing at the birthday party?
They just hummed because they didn't know the words.

'What's green and slimy with pink spots and three eyes on stalks?'
'I don't know.'
'Neither do I, but one of them's just started eating your birthday cake!'

'We're having musical soup on my birthday.'
'How's that?'
'It's going to be piping hot.'

What wobbles and flies at birthday parties?
A jellycopter.

Why should you wear a tartan waistcoat on your birthday?
To keep your tummy in check.

Why did the apple turn over?
Because it saw the jam roll.

What did one strawberry say to the other?
'What a jam we're both in.'

Do you know the joke about butter?
I'd better not tell you, you might spread it.

What do policemen like to eat at birthday parties?
Truncheon meat.

What's a frog's favourite drink?
Croak-a-cola.

What do hedgehogs like on their birthdays?
Prickled onions.

What's bad-tempered and goes with custard?
Apple grumble.

What did the cookie say to the biscuit?
Crumbs.

What's green and bounces?
A spring onion.

What happened to the prunes who were in a stew?
They were taken into custardy.

Which hand should you stir your tea with?
Well, it's better to use a spoon.

What crisps fly at birthday parties?
Plane crisps.

How can you make a sloth fast?
Take his food away.

What did the hamburger say to the tomato?
That's enough of your sauce.

What's the best thing to eat with jacket potatoes?
Button mushrooms.

How do people eat cheese in Wales?
Caerphilly.

What did the orange squash say to the glass of water?
I'm diluted to meet you.

What's the rudest food?
Sausages – because they spit when you fry them.

Why did the man have a sausage stuck behind his ear?
He'd just eaten his pencil.

Why would you never be hungry at the beach?
Because of the sand which is there.

Why did the jelly wobble?
Because it saw the milk shake.

What cheese is made backwards?
Edam.

Why did the ice cream?
Because the biscuit was a wafer so long.

What jam can't you spread?
Traffic jam.

What's white and fluffy and always comes back when you throw it?
Boomeringue.

What did the biscuits say to the almonds?
'You're nuts, we're crackers.'

Why shouldn't you give tea to an elephant?
He might get a little trunk.

What do tight-rope walkers eat on their birthdays?
Anything, so long as it's a balanced meal.

What do polar bears like to eat on their birthdays?
Iceburgers.

What sweets do polar bears like on their birthdays?
Glacier mints.

What's brown and prickly and squirts jam at you?
A hedgehog eating a doughnut.

What do ghosts like eating at birthday parties?
Ghoulash, washed down with demonade.

What sweets do frogs like for their birthdays?
Lollihops.

What do cats like at their birthday parties?
Jellyfish.

CAKES & CANDLES

What did the candles on the birthday cake say?
'Let's all go out together.'

What's yellow and swings from cake to cake?
Tarzipan.

Why are cooks bullies?
They whip the cream and beat the eggs.

What did the birthday cake say when the candles were put on it?
'Well, blow me.'

What cake gives you an electric shock?
A currant cake.

What's the best thing to put into a birthday cake?
Your teeth.

What's purple and burns cakes?
Alfred the Grape.

What bird makes its own birthday cakes?
A cook-oo.

What cake shouldn't you eat?
A cake of soap.

When is a birthday cake musical?
When it's got I-sing on it.

Why did the man eat the candles on his birthday cake?
He only wanted a light meal.

What did the flour say when it fell over?
'It's all right, I'm self-raising.'

What do you do with a dentist's birthday cake?
Let him put in the filling.

What did the cat feel like after eating her birthday cake?
Purrfectly satisfied.

What has pink icing, candles and flies?
A stale birthday cake.

What has icing, candles and can break planks of wood?
Extra-tough birthday cake.

Why is a bad boxer like a candle?
One blow and he's out.

What sort of cake do you *not* want on your birthday?
Stomach-ache.

Which side of a birthday cake is the left side?
The side that hasn't been eaten.

What happened when Frankenstein swallowed his birthday cake all in one go?
He needed shock treatment – it was a currant cake.

What can a whole birthday cake do that half a birthday cake can't?
Look round.

What do you use to make a birthday cake for your dog?
Collie-flour.

What's round, has candles and hums?
An electric birthday cake.

Have you heard the joke about the two-ton birthday cake?
It takes some swallowing.

'How many more times have I got to tell you to stop nibbling that birthday cake?'
'No more, Mum, it's all gone.'

'Mum, can I have two pieces of birthday cake, please?
'Certainly – take this piece and cut it in two.'

Dan: This match won't light.
Billy: That's funny, it did this morning.

What happened at the dragon's birthday party?
When he blew on the cake he relit all the candles!

What did the vampire say when he was given a piece of birthday cake?
Fangs for this.

How do elves make birthday cakes?
With elf-raising flour.

Which burns longer, a pink candle or a blue candle?
Neither – they both burn shorter.

Granny: What would you like?
Lucy: Birthday cake.
Granny: Birthday cake what?
Lucy: Birthday cake first.

What has icing and candles and gradually changes from pink to blue?
A birthday cake holding its breath.

What has icing and candles and hums?
A birthday cake that doesn't know the words.

How was the birthday cake when all the candles were blown out in one go?
De-lighted.

What do you do with a blue birthday cake?
Try and cheer it up.

Who invented candles on birthday cakes?
Some bright spark.

Emma: My mum's making me an Enthusiasm cake for my birthday.
Kate: Why's it called Enthusiasm cake?
Emma: She puts everything she's got into it.

'Is it true you like birthday cake?'
'Yes, it's a consuming passion.'

'Did you like your birthday cake, George?'
'Yes, I'm internally grateful.'

'Don't keep reaching across the table, Sarah – haven't you got a tongue in your head?'
'Yes, but my arm's longer.'

What has icing and candles and goes round and round?
A long-playing birthday cake.

In which tree might you find a birthday cake?
A pantry.

What's a chicken's favourite birthday cake?
A layer cake.

What is very large, has candles, icing and tusks?
A mammoth birthday cake!

Sam: What's the difference between a birthday cake and a mud pie?
Ben: I don't know.
Sam: Well, in that case I'll eat the birthday cake and you can have the mud pie.

'Have you ever seen a man-eating tiger?'
'*No, but I've seen a man eating birthday cake.*'

HIPPO BIRTHDAY

Knock, knock.
Who's there?
Hippo.
Hippo who?
Hippo birthday to you!

Where does a two-ton hippo sit at your birthday party?
Anywhere he wants to!

What are you least likely to find in a bath with a hippo?
The bath water.

What do you give a hippo on board ship?
A wide berth.

Why did the hippo wait under the palm tree?
He wanted a birthday date.

Why did it take the giraffe so long to apologize to the hippo?
It took him a long time to swallow his pride.

Why don't hippos like penguins at their birthday parties?
They can't get the wrappers off.

What's the difference between a hippo and a post-box?
You don't know? Well I shan't send you to post a letter.

Why did the hippo jump in the river?
He wanted to splash out on his mum's birthday.

What would you do if a hippo sat in front of you at the cinema?
Miss most of the film.

1st hippo: This coffee is delicious, it tastes like mud!
2nd hippo: That's because it was ground this morning.

What happened when the hippo got jelly and custard in his ears?
He became a trifle deaf.

Why did the hippo keep bread in his comic?
He liked crumby jokes.

How did seven hippos fit under one umbrella and not get wet?
It wasn't raining.

What game do hippos like playing at birthday parties?
Squash.

Knock, knock.
Who's there?
Mini.
Mini who?
Mini hippo returns!

BIRTHDAY GIFTS

What's the best thing to give a budgie for his birthday?
A birthday tweet.

Where do you get a birthday present for your dog?
British Bone Stores.

Where do you get a birthday present for your cat?
From a catalogue.

What's the best thing to give a goldfish for his birthday?
A ticket to the Super Bowl.

What do you always get on your birthday?
A year older.

What's the best way to make your birthday money go a long way?
Post it to Australia.

What did the thief give his girlfriend for her birthday?
A stole.

Did you hear about the boy who wanted budgie-seed for his birthday?
He wanted to grow his own budgie.

What should you do if your budgie is stolen?
Call the Flying Squad.

'Come here, you naughty boy. I'll teach you to eat your sister's birthday chocolates.'
'*It's all right, Dad. I already know how.*'

Susan: What did you get for your birthday?
Jane: A mouth-organ. it's the best present I ever got.
Susan: Why?
Jane: My mother gives me twenty pence a week not to blow it.

What does a polar bear like for his birthday?
Iced lolly.

Where did Dracula put his birthday money?
In a blood bank.

Would you like to hear the joke about the enormous birthday parcel?
There's nothing in it!

Why did the boy want a snake for his birthday?
He wanted an adder to help with his homework.

Tom got a dog for his birthday and called it Camera.
It was always snapping.

Shall I tell you the joke about the boy who only got a pencil for his birthday.
There's no point.

My sister's a person of rare gifts.
The last time she gave me a birthday
present was three years ago.

Sarah: Here's your birthday present – a
box of your favourite chocolates.
Julia: Ooo – thanks. But it's half empty.
Sarah: Well, they're my favourite
chocolates too.

What do you give someone who has
everything?
Penicillin.

'Dad, Billy's just eaten the clock I gave him
for his birthday.'
'How was that?'
'He found it very time-consuming.'

What do you give a deaf fishmonger for his birthday?
A herring-aid.

Where can you buy a birthday present for a plumber?
In Bath.

Where can you buy a birthday present for a gardener?
In Barrow.

Where's the best place to get a birthday present for someone in prison?
At Liberty's.

Where would you buy a birthday present
for Superman?
At a supermarket.

What did the witch want for her birthday?
A witch watch.

What did the wizard want for his birthday?
A spell at the seaside.

Where did the weatherman go for his birthday treat?
Hayling Island.

What's the best thing to give as a parting gift?
A comb.

'Mum, I'm writing a thank-you letter to Grandad.'
'Good, but your handwriting seems very large.'
'Well, Grandad's deaf, so I'm writing loud.'

What did the pig do with his birthday money?
Put it in a piggy-bank.

Where do you get a birthday present for an elephant?
At the Over-size shop.

Where do you get a birthday present for your tortoise?
At a Shell Service Station.

A BIRTHDAY QUIZ

What suit do you wear in the bath?
Your birthday suit!

How did the burglar manage to steal the birthday tea?
He found it was a piece of cake.

What sits in a fruit bowl and shouts for help?
A damson in distress.

If you meet a crocodile on your birthday what time is it?
Time to run.

How do you hire a horse for a birthday treat?
Put four bricks under him.

What happens if the Queen burps at her birthday party?
She issues a Royal Pardon.

What do you call a train loaded with toffee?
A chew-chew train.

What never looks right?
Your left ear.

Where do you buy a birthday present for Tarzan?
At a jungle sale.

How many seconds are there in a year?
Twelve. January 2nd, February 2nd . . .

What did the birthday card say to the stamp?
Stick with me and we'll go places.

Why do bald men spend their birthdays outside?
They need some fresh hair.

What do you call two rows of cabbages?
A dual cabbage-way.

What can you eat in Paris, as a birthday treat?
The Trifle Tower.

What did the cannibal say to the jungle explorer?
'Dr Livingstone, I consume.'

What do you call an ant celebrating his 100th birthday?
Antique.

What do you call a camel with three humps?
Humphrey.

Where were chips first fried?
In Greece.

How do you make a potato puff?
Chase it round the garden.

What do you give a sick lemon?
Lemonade.

What stays hot, even in the fridge?
Mustard.

Which letters are not in the alphabet?
The ones in the post-box.

What's the hardest thing about learning to ride a bike?
The pavement.

What nut sounds like a sneeze?
A cashew.

What is the largest mouse in the world?
A hippopotamouse.

What did the crook get when he stole the calendar?
Twelve months.

What travels the world but stays in a corner?
A postage stamp.

What invention enables you to see through the thickest walls?
The window.

Why are wolves like playing-cards?
They come in packs.

What animal has the highest intelligence?
The giraffe.

What exams are horses good at?
Hay levels.

What pet makes the loudest noise?
A trumpet.

If a buttercup is yellow what colour is a hiccup?
Burple.

What vegetables do you get in boats?
Leeks.

When is water not water?
When it's dripping.

What do you get if you cross a sweet with a bird?
A fudgerigar.

What do you get if you cross a pig with a zebra?
Striped sausages.

What do jelly babies wear in the rain?
Gumboots.

What's brave, handsome and has a very bad memory?
Errr . . . I can't remember.

Why do people study blotting paper?
It's an absorbing subject.

Two tomatoes were crossing a road. When one reached the other side first, what did he say?
"Come on! Ketch – up!"

What happened when a hundred wigs were stolen?
Police combed the area.

Why was the crab arrested?
He kept pinching things.

How do you make a Mexican chilli?
Take him to the North Pole.

Why did the robber take a bath?
So he could make a clean get-away.

Why did the boy tiptoe past the chemist?
So that he didn't wake the sleeping pills.

What happened when the cat swallowed a penny?
There was money in the kitty.

Why did the chewing gum cross the road?
Because it was stuck to the chicken's foot.

What is an Ig?
An eskimo's house without a toilet.

Man: Doctor, Doctor, I feel like a bridge.
Doctor: What's come over you?
Man: Two cars, a van and a lorry.

What do you get if you cross a cow with a sheep with a baby goat?
The Milky Bar Kid, of course.

DAFT DITTIES

Mary had a little lamb
It was her birthday treat.
She wolfed the lot in half-an-hour
Then wanted more to eat.

Mary had a little lamb
It was a birthday gift.
She taught it how to biff and box —
It nearly alwaves miffed.

Little Miss Muffet
Sat on a tuffet
Eating her birthday cake
When along came some mice
Who all wanted a slice –
Now they've all got the tummy ache.

Old King Cole
Was a merry old soul
And he called for his fiddlers *two*.
And they came in a trice
And played for him twice:
'A VERY HAPPY BIRTHDAY TO YOU!'